50 New Zealand Cuisine Recipes for Home

By: Kelly Johnson

Table of Contents

- Pavlova
- Kiwi Burger
- Hangi
- Hokey Pokey Ice Cream
- Whitebait Fritters
- Paua Fritters
- ANZAC Biscuits
- Lolly Cake
- Pork and Puha
- Rewena Bread
- Mussel Fritters
- Boil Up
- Māori Fried Bread
- Whitebait Patties
- Kumara Chips
- Mince and Cheese Pie
- Kiwi Lamb Chops
- Hāngī Pie
- Kiwi Meatloaf
- Seafood Chowder
- Cheese Rolls
- Māori Boil-Up
- Bacon and Egg Pie
- Kiwi Dip
- Kiwi Onion Dip
- Kiwi Bacon and Egg Pie
- Māori Fried Bread
- Kiwi Sausage Rolls
- Kiwi Potato Salad
- Green-Lipped Mussel Soup
- Kiwi Crayfish Salad
- Kiwi Garlic Prawns
- Kiwi Salmon Pie
- Kiwi Venison Stew
- Kiwi Fish and Chips

- Kiwi Hangi Parcels
- Kiwi Roast Lamb
- Kiwi Lamb Shank Soup
- Kiwi Mussel Soup
- Kiwi Smoked Fish Pie
- Kiwi Spaghetti on Toast
- Kiwi Muttonbird Pie
- Kiwi Roast Beef
- Kiwi Roast Chicken
- Kiwi Bacon-Wrapped Sausages
- Kiwi Fish Pie
- Kiwi Beef Stew
- Kiwi Cheese and Bacon Roll
- Kiwi Fried Paua
- Kiwi Chocolate Fish

Pavlova

Ingredients:

- 4 large egg whites, at room temperature
- 1 cup caster sugar
- 1 teaspoon white vinegar
- 1 teaspoon cornflour
- 1 teaspoon vanilla extract
- 1 cup whipped cream
- Fresh fruits (such as kiwi, strawberries, and passionfruit) for topping

Instructions:

1. Preheat your oven to 150°C (300°F). Line a baking tray with parchment paper.
2. In a clean, dry mixing bowl, beat the egg whites using an electric mixer on medium speed until soft peaks form.
3. Gradually add the caster sugar, one tablespoon at a time, while continuing to beat on high speed. Make sure the sugar is fully dissolved and the mixture is glossy. This might take about 10 minutes.
4. Once all the sugar has been added and the mixture is thick and glossy, add the vinegar, cornflour, and vanilla extract. Gently fold them into the mixture using a spatula.
5. Spoon the mixture onto the prepared baking tray, forming a round mound. Use the spatula to shape it into a circle with slightly raised edges.
6. Place the pavlova in the preheated oven and immediately reduce the temperature to 120°C (250°F). Bake for 1 hour and 15 minutes, or until the pavlova is crisp on the outside and slightly soft in the center.
7. Turn off the oven and leave the pavlova to cool completely with the oven door slightly ajar.
8. Once cooled, carefully transfer the pavlova to a serving plate. Top with whipped cream and fresh fruits of your choice.
9. Serve immediately and enjoy your delicious Pavlova!

Kiwi Burger

Ingredients:

- 500g ground beef
- Salt and pepper, to taste
- 4 hamburger buns
- Butter, for toasting
- Lettuce leaves
- Tomato slices
- Red onion slices
- Pickles
- 4 slices of cheddar cheese
- 4 slices of cooked beetroot
- 4 fried eggs
- Tomato sauce (ketchup) or your preferred burger sauce

Instructions:

1. Divide the ground beef into 4 equal portions and shape them into burger patties. Season each patty with salt and pepper.
2. Heat a grill or frying pan over medium-high heat. Cook the burger patties for about 4-5 minutes on each side, or until they reach your desired level of doneness. In the last minute of cooking, place a slice of cheddar cheese on each patty to melt.
3. While the patties are cooking, lightly toast the hamburger buns in a separate pan with a little butter.
4. Assemble the burgers: Place a lettuce leaf on the bottom half of each bun, followed by a tomato slice, onion slices, pickles, and a slice of cooked beetroot.
5. Place a cooked burger patty with melted cheese on top of the beetroot.
6. Fry the eggs in a pan until the whites are set but the yolks are still runny. Place a fried egg on top of each burger patty.
7. Drizzle tomato sauce or your preferred burger sauce over the eggs.
8. Top with the other half of the toasted bun and serve immediately.

Enjoy your Kiwi Burger, complete with its unique and delicious combination of flavors!

Hangi

Ingredients:

- 1-2 kg of meat (such as lamb, pork, chicken, or beef)
- Root vegetables (such as potatoes, kumara/sweet potatoes, carrots)
- Seasoning (salt, pepper, herbs, etc.)
- Aluminum foil

Instructions:

1. Prepare your meat and vegetables: Cut the meat into large pieces and peel and chop the vegetables into chunks.
2. Season the meat and vegetables with salt, pepper, and any other desired seasonings. You can also marinate the meat if preferred.
3. Preheat your oven to a low temperature, around 120-150°C (250-300°F).
4. Take heavy-duty aluminum foil and layer it to create parcels for the meat and vegetables. Ensure they are tightly sealed to trap steam inside.
5. Place a layer of rocks in the bottom of a roasting pan or large baking dish. These rocks will act as the heated stones in the Hangi.
6. Arrange the foil parcels on top of the rocks in a single layer. Make sure there is enough space between each parcel for steam to circulate.
7. Cover the entire roasting pan or baking dish tightly with aluminum foil, sealing in the steam.
8. Place the covered dish in the preheated oven and allow the meat and vegetables to cook slowly for several hours. Cooking time will vary depending on the size and type of meat and vegetables used. Aim for at least 3-4 hours of cooking time for the flavors to develop and the meat to become tender.
9. Once cooked, carefully remove the parcels from the oven and let them rest for a few minutes before opening.
10. Carefully open the parcels, being cautious of the steam, and transfer the cooked meat and vegetables to a serving platter.
11. Serve hot, and enjoy the delicious flavors of your homemade Hangi-style meal!

While this method may not be as traditional as the underground pit oven, it still captures the essence of Hangi cooking and produces tender, flavorful meat and vegetables.

Hokey Pokey Ice Cream

Ingredients:

For the Hokey Pokey Toffee:

- 1/2 cup (100g) granulated sugar
- 2 tablespoons golden syrup (or corn syrup)
- 1 teaspoon baking soda

For the Ice Cream:

- 2 cups heavy cream
- 1 cup whole milk
- 3/4 cup granulated sugar
- 1 teaspoon vanilla extract

Instructions:

1. Start by making the hokey pokey toffee. Line a baking sheet with parchment paper and set aside.
2. In a medium saucepan, combine the sugar and golden syrup over medium heat. Stir constantly until the sugar has dissolved.
3. Once the sugar has dissolved, stop stirring and allow the mixture to boil until it turns a golden caramel color, about 5-7 minutes. Be careful not to let it burn.
4. Remove the saucepan from heat and quickly stir in the baking soda. The mixture will foam up.
5. Immediately pour the foaming toffee onto the prepared baking sheet. Allow it to cool and harden completely, then break it into small, bite-sized pieces.
6. In a separate bowl, whisk together the heavy cream, milk, sugar, and vanilla extract until the sugar is dissolved and the mixture is smooth.
7. Pour the ice cream mixture into an ice cream maker and churn according to the manufacturer's instructions until it reaches a soft-serve consistency.
8. Once the ice cream is ready, quickly fold in the hokey pokey toffee pieces until evenly distributed.

9. Transfer the ice cream to a freezer-safe container and freeze for several hours or overnight until firm.
10. Serve the hokey pokey ice cream scoops in cones or bowls, and enjoy the delightful combination of creamy vanilla ice cream and crunchy toffee!

This homemade version captures the classic flavors of New Zealand's Hokey Pokey Ice Cream and is sure to be a hit with friends and family.

Whitebait Fritters

Ingredients:

- 200g fresh whitebait
- 2 large eggs
- 2 tablespoons all-purpose flour
- Salt and pepper, to taste
- Butter or oil for frying
- Lemon wedges, for serving (optional)

Instructions:

1. Start by gently rinsing the whitebait under cold water and patting them dry with paper towels. Be careful not to break them apart as they are delicate.
2. In a mixing bowl, lightly beat the eggs. Add the flour and season with salt and pepper. Stir until well combined.
3. Gently fold the whitebait into the egg mixture until evenly coated.
4. Heat a non-stick frying pan over medium heat and add a knob of butter or a splash of oil.
5. Once the butter is melted or the oil is heated, spoon the whitebait mixture into the pan to form small fritters. You can make them as large or as small as you prefer.
6. Cook the fritters for 1-2 minutes on each side, or until they are golden brown and crispy. Be careful not to overcrowd the pan; you may need to cook them in batches.
7. Use a spatula to carefully flip the fritters and cook on the other side until golden brown and cooked through.
8. Once cooked, transfer the fritters to a plate lined with paper towels to drain any excess oil.
9. Serve the whitebait fritters hot, with lemon wedges on the side for squeezing over the top, if desired.

Enjoy these delicious whitebait fritters as a snack, appetizer, or part of a meal. They're best enjoyed fresh and hot!

Paua Fritters

Ingredients:

- 250g fresh or canned paua (abalone), finely chopped
- 2 large eggs
- 1/2 cup all-purpose flour
- 1/4 cup milk
- 1/4 cup finely chopped onion
- 1/4 cup finely chopped parsley
- Salt and pepper, to taste
- Butter or oil for frying
- Lemon wedges, for serving (optional)

Instructions:

1. If using fresh paua, ensure it has been thoroughly cleaned and tenderized before chopping it finely. If using canned paua, drain it well.
2. In a mixing bowl, beat the eggs lightly. Add the flour and milk, and whisk until you have a smooth batter.
3. Stir in the chopped paua, onion, parsley, salt, and pepper, ensuring the ingredients are evenly distributed throughout the batter.
4. Heat a non-stick frying pan over medium heat and add a knob of butter or a splash of oil.
5. Once the butter is melted or the oil is heated, spoon the paua batter into the pan to form small fritters. You can make them as large or as small as you prefer.
6. Cook the fritters for 2-3 minutes on each side, or until they are golden brown and cooked through.
7. Use a spatula to carefully flip the fritters and cook on the other side until golden brown and cooked through.
8. Once cooked, transfer the fritters to a plate lined with paper towels to drain any excess oil.
9. Serve the paua fritters hot, with lemon wedges on the side for squeezing over the top, if desired.

Enjoy these delicious paua fritters as a snack, appetizer, or part of a meal. They're best enjoyed fresh and hot!

ANZAC Biscuits

Ingredients:

- 1 cup rolled oats
- 1 cup desiccated coconut
- 1 cup all-purpose flour
- 1 cup granulated sugar
- 125g (1/2 cup) unsalted butter
- 2 tablespoons golden syrup or honey
- 1 teaspoon baking soda
- 2 tablespoons boiling water

Instructions:

1. Preheat your oven to 160°C (320°F) and line a baking tray with parchment paper.
2. In a large mixing bowl, combine the rolled oats, desiccated coconut, flour, and sugar.
3. In a small saucepan, melt the butter and golden syrup together over low heat, stirring until smooth and well combined.
4. In a small bowl, mix the baking soda with the boiling water until dissolved.
5. Add the baking soda mixture to the melted butter and golden syrup mixture. The mixture will foam up slightly.
6. Pour the wet ingredients into the dry ingredients and stir until well combined and the mixture forms a dough.
7. Take tablespoons of the dough and roll them into balls. Place them on the prepared baking tray, leaving some space between each ball for spreading.
8. Use your fingers or a fork to gently flatten each ball of dough.
9. Bake the ANZAC biscuits in the preheated oven for 12-15 minutes, or until golden brown.
10. Remove the biscuits from the oven and allow them to cool on the baking tray for a few minutes before transferring them to a wire rack to cool completely.
11. Once cooled, store the ANZAC biscuits in an airtight container at room temperature for up to a week.

Enjoy these delicious ANZAC biscuits with a cup of tea or coffee, or as a sweet snack any time of the day!

Lolly Cake

Ingredients:

- 250g malt biscuits (such as Griffins Malt or Marie biscuits)
- 100g butter
- 200g sweetened condensed milk
- 150g fruit-flavored sweets (such as Eskimos or Fruit Puffs), chopped into small pieces
- Desiccated coconut, for rolling (optional)

Instructions:

1. Place the malt biscuits in a resealable plastic bag and crush them into small pieces using a rolling pin or the back of a spoon. Alternatively, you can pulse them in a food processor until finely crushed. Transfer the crushed biscuits to a large mixing bowl.
2. In a small saucepan, melt the butter over low heat.
3. Once the butter is melted, add the sweetened condensed milk to the saucepan and stir until well combined. Heat gently until the mixture is smooth and combined.
4. Pour the melted butter and condensed milk mixture over the crushed biscuits in the mixing bowl. Add the chopped fruit-flavored sweets.
5. Use a spatula or wooden spoon to mix all the ingredients together until well combined and the biscuit crumbs are evenly coated.
6. Line a small loaf tin or rectangular dish with parchment paper or cling film, leaving some overhang on the sides for easy removal.
7. Transfer the mixture into the lined tin and press it down firmly and evenly using the back of a spoon or your fingers.
8. If desired, sprinkle desiccated coconut over the top of the lolly cake for decoration.
9. Cover the tin with cling film and refrigerate the lolly cake for at least 2-3 hours, or until firm and set.
10. Once set, remove the lolly cake from the tin using the overhanging parchment paper or cling film. Place it on a cutting board and cut into slices or squares to serve.
11. Enjoy your homemade Lolly Cake as a sweet treat or dessert! Store any leftovers in an airtight container in the refrigerator for up to one week.

Lolly Cake is a nostalgic and fun dessert that's perfect for sharing with family and friends.

Pork and Puha

Ingredients:

- 500g pork belly or pork shoulder, diced
- 1 bunch of puha leaves, washed and roughly chopped (substitute with watercress or spinach if puha is unavailable)
- 1 onion, finely chopped
- 2 cloves garlic, minced
- 1 tablespoon cooking oil
- Salt and pepper, to taste
- Water or broth, as needed

Instructions:

1. Heat the cooking oil in a large skillet or frying pan over medium heat.
2. Add the diced pork to the pan and cook until browned on all sides, stirring occasionally.
3. Once the pork is browned, add the chopped onion and minced garlic to the pan. Cook for a few minutes until the onion is softened and fragrant.
4. Season the pork and onion mixture with salt and pepper to taste.
5. Add enough water or broth to the pan to cover the pork. Bring the liquid to a simmer.
6. Reduce the heat to low, cover the pan, and let the pork simmer gently for about 1 to 1 1/2 hours, or until the pork is tender and cooked through. Stir occasionally and add more liquid if needed to prevent the mixture from drying out.
7. Once the pork is cooked, add the chopped puha leaves to the pan. If using spinach or watercress, add them at this stage as well.
8. Stir the puha leaves into the pork mixture and continue to simmer for another 5-10 minutes, or until the puha is wilted and tender.
9. Taste and adjust the seasoning if necessary.
10. Once the pork and puha are cooked and flavored to your liking, remove the pan from the heat.
11. Serve the pork and puha hot, accompanied by steamed rice, mashed potatoes, or your favorite side dishes.

Enjoy this traditional Māori dish of pork and puha as a hearty and flavorful meal, perfect for sharing with family and friends.

Rewena Bread

Ingredients:

For the Rewena (Starter):

- 2 medium-sized potatoes, peeled and grated
- 1 cup warm water
- 1 teaspoon sugar
- 1 teaspoon active dry yeast

For the Bread Dough:

- 4 cups all-purpose flour
- 1 teaspoon salt
- 1/2 cup warm water
- 2 tablespoons sugar
- 1/4 cup melted butter or oil

Instructions:

1. Start by making the Rewena (Starter):
    - In a large mixing bowl, combine the grated potatoes, warm water, sugar, and yeast. Stir until well combined.
    - Cover the bowl loosely with a clean kitchen towel or plastic wrap and leave it in a warm place for 2-3 days, stirring occasionally. The mixture should develop a slightly sour smell and become bubbly.
2. Once the Rewena is ready, it's time to make the bread dough:
    - In a large mixing bowl, combine the flour and salt.
    - In a separate bowl, dissolve the sugar in warm water, then add the melted butter or oil.
    - Add the prepared Rewena (starter) to the flour mixture and mix well.
    - Gradually add the sugar-water mixture to the flour mixture, stirring until a soft dough forms.
3. Turn the dough out onto a lightly floured surface and knead for 5-10 minutes, or until the dough is smooth and elastic.

4. Place the dough in a greased bowl, cover with a clean kitchen towel or plastic wrap, and let it rise in a warm place for 1-2 hours, or until doubled in size.
5. Once the dough has risen, punch it down to release the air, then shape it into a loaf or round loaf.
6. Place the shaped dough on a greased baking sheet or in a greased loaf pan. Cover it again and let it rise for another 30-45 minutes.
7. Preheat your oven to 180°C (350°F).
8. Bake the bread in the preheated oven for 30-40 minutes, or until golden brown and cooked through. If baking in a loaf pan, the bread should sound hollow when tapped on the bottom.
9. Once baked, remove the bread from the oven and let it cool on a wire rack before slicing and serving.

Enjoy your homemade Rewena Bread with butter, jam, or your favorite spreads. It's delicious served warm or toasted!

Mussel Fritters

Ingredients:

- 500g fresh mussels (or canned mussels)
- 1 cup all-purpose flour
- 1 teaspoon baking powder
- 2 eggs
- 1/4 cup milk
- 1/4 cup chopped fresh parsley
- Salt and pepper, to taste
- Cooking oil, for frying
- Lemon wedges, for serving (optional)

Instructions:

1. If using fresh mussels, clean them thoroughly by scrubbing the shells and removing any beards or debris. Discard any mussels that are open or do not close when tapped.
2. Steam the fresh mussels until they open, then remove the meat from the shells and roughly chop them. If using canned mussels, drain them well.
3. In a large mixing bowl, sift together the flour and baking powder.
4. In a separate bowl, beat the eggs and milk together until well combined.
5. Gradually pour the egg mixture into the flour mixture, stirring constantly until you have a smooth batter.
6. Add the chopped mussels and chopped parsley to the batter, and season with salt and pepper to taste. Stir until the mussels and parsley are evenly distributed throughout the batter.
7. Heat a little cooking oil in a frying pan over medium heat.
8. Once the oil is hot, spoon dollops of the mussel batter into the pan to form fritters. Use the back of the spoon to flatten them slightly.
9. Cook the fritters for 2-3 minutes on each side, or until golden brown and cooked through. You may need to cook them in batches depending on the size of your pan.
10. Once cooked, remove the fritters from the pan and drain them on paper towels to remove any excess oil.

11. Serve the mussel fritters hot, with lemon wedges on the side for squeezing over the top, if desired.

Enjoy these delicious mussel fritters as a tasty appetizer or main dish, perfect for seafood lovers!

Boil Up

Ingredients:

- 500g pork bones or pork shoulder, chopped into pieces
- 1 onion, peeled and quartered
- 2 carrots, peeled and chopped into chunks
- 2 potatoes, peeled and chopped into chunks
- 1-2 cups chopped cabbage or other leafy greens (such as spinach or silverbeet)
- Salt, to taste
- Water, enough to cover the ingredients in the pot

Optional:

- Kumara (sweet potato), peeled and chopped into chunks
- Pumpkin, peeled and chopped into chunks
- Dumplings (made from self-raising flour and water)

Instructions:

1. In a large pot or Dutch oven, add the pork bones or pork shoulder pieces and cover them with water.
2. Bring the pot to a boil over medium-high heat, then reduce the heat to low and simmer for about 1-2 hours, or until the pork is tender and cooked through. Skim off any foam or impurities that rise to the surface during cooking.
3. Once the pork is cooked, add the onion, carrots, and potatoes to the pot. If using, add the kumara and pumpkin as well.
4. Simmer the vegetables with the pork for about 20-30 minutes, or until they are tender.
5. Add the chopped cabbage or leafy greens to the pot and simmer for an additional 5-10 minutes, or until wilted.
6. Season the Boil Up with salt to taste, adjusting the seasoning as needed.
7. If desired, add dumplings to the pot during the last 10-15 minutes of cooking. To make dumplings, simply mix together self-raising flour and enough water to form a stiff dough. Divide the dough into small balls and drop them into the simmering broth.

8. Once the vegetables are tender and the dumplings are cooked through, remove the pot from the heat.
9. Serve the Boil Up hot, ladled into bowls with plenty of the flavorful broth.

Enjoy this comforting and hearty Boil Up as a delicious meal, perfect for warming up on a chilly day!

Māori Fried Bread

Ingredients:

- 2 cups all-purpose flour
- 2 teaspoons baking powder
- 1/2 teaspoon salt
- 1 tablespoon sugar
- Warm water (approximately 1 cup)
- Cooking oil, for frying

Instructions:

1. In a large mixing bowl, sift together the flour, baking powder, salt, and sugar.
2. Gradually add warm water to the dry ingredients, stirring with a spoon or your hands to form a soft dough. Start with about 3/4 cup of water and add more as needed until the dough comes together.
3. Turn the dough out onto a lightly floured surface and knead it for a few minutes until it becomes smooth and elastic.
4. Divide the dough into equal-sized portions, depending on how large you want your fried bread to be. Roll each portion into a ball and then flatten it slightly with your hands to form a disc.
5. Heat cooking oil in a frying pan or skillet over medium heat. The oil should be hot but not smoking.
6. Carefully place the flattened dough discs into the hot oil, one or two at a time, depending on the size of your pan. Fry the bread for 2-3 minutes on each side, or until golden brown and cooked through.
7. Use tongs or a slotted spoon to transfer the fried bread to a plate lined with paper towels to drain any excess oil.
8. Serve the Māori fried bread hot, either plain or with your favorite toppings such as butter, jam, honey, or savory spreads.
9. Enjoy your delicious homemade Māori fried bread as a snack, side dish, or part of a meal!

Māori fried bread is versatile and can be enjoyed in various ways. It's a comfort food that's perfect for sharing with family and friends.

Whitebait Patties

Ingredients:

- 200g fresh whitebait
- 2 eggs
- 2 tablespoons all-purpose flour
- Salt and pepper, to taste
- Butter or oil for frying
- Lemon wedges, for serving (optional)

Instructions:

1. Start by rinsing the fresh whitebait under cold water and patting them dry with paper towels. Be gentle as whitebait are delicate.
2. In a mixing bowl, lightly beat the eggs. Add the flour, salt, and pepper, and whisk until well combined.
3. Gently fold the whitebait into the egg mixture until evenly coated.
4. Heat a non-stick frying pan over medium heat and add a knob of butter or a splash of oil.
5. Once the butter is melted or the oil is heated, spoon the whitebait mixture into the pan to form small patties. You can make them as large or as small as you prefer.
6. Cook the patties for 1-2 minutes on each side, or until they are golden brown and crispy. Be careful not to overcrowd the pan; you may need to cook them in batches.
7. Use a spatula to carefully flip the patties and cook on the other side until golden brown and cooked through.
8. Once cooked, transfer the patties to a plate lined with paper towels to drain any excess oil.
9. Serve the whitebait patties hot, with lemon wedges on the side for squeezing over the top, if desired.

Enjoy these delicious whitebait patties as a snack, appetizer, or part of a meal. They're best enjoyed fresh and hot!

Kumara Chips

Ingredients:

- 2 large kumara (sweet potatoes)
- 2 tablespoons olive oil
- Salt and pepper, to taste
- Optional seasonings: paprika, garlic powder, rosemary, or any other preferred herbs and spices

Instructions:

1. Preheat your oven to 200°C (400°F) and line a baking sheet with parchment paper or aluminum foil.
2. Peel the kumara and cut them into thin strips, similar in size to traditional potato fries.
3. In a large bowl, toss the kumara strips with olive oil until they are evenly coated.
4. Season the kumara strips with salt, pepper, and any additional seasonings of your choice, such as paprika, garlic powder, or rosemary. Toss to coat evenly.
5. Arrange the seasoned kumara strips in a single layer on the prepared baking sheet, making sure they are not overcrowded.
6. Bake the kumara chips in the preheated oven for 20-25 minutes, flipping them halfway through the cooking time, until they are golden brown and crispy.
7. Once cooked, remove the kumara chips from the oven and let them cool slightly before serving.
8. Serve the kumara chips hot, as a delicious and healthy snack or side dish.

Enjoy your homemade kumara chips with your favorite dipping sauce, such as aioli, ketchup, or sweet chili sauce. They're crispy, flavorful, and addictive!

Mince and Cheese Pie

Ingredients:

For the Filling:

- 500g minced beef or lamb
- 1 onion, finely chopped
- 2 cloves garlic, minced
- 1 carrot, grated
- 1 tablespoon tomato paste
- 1 tablespoon Worcestershire sauce
- 1 teaspoon dried mixed herbs (such as thyme, rosemary, and oregano)
- Salt and pepper, to taste
- 1/2 cup beef or vegetable broth
- 1 tablespoon olive oil

For the Pie:

- 2 sheets of store-bought puff pastry, thawed
- 1 cup grated cheese (cheddar or your preferred cheese)

Instructions:

1. Preheat your oven to 200°C (400°F) and grease a pie dish or baking dish.
2. In a large skillet or frying pan, heat the olive oil over medium heat. Add the chopped onion and garlic and cook until softened and fragrant, about 3-4 minutes.
3. Add the minced meat to the pan and cook, breaking it up with a spoon, until browned and cooked through.
4. Stir in the grated carrot, tomato paste, Worcestershire sauce, dried herbs, salt, and pepper. Cook for another 2-3 minutes, allowing the flavors to meld together.
5. Pour in the beef or vegetable broth and simmer the mixture for 5-10 minutes, or until the liquid has reduced and the filling has thickened slightly. Remove from heat and let it cool slightly.

6. While the filling is cooling, prepare the pastry. Roll out one sheet of puff pastry and line the bottom of the greased pie dish with it. Trim any excess pastry hanging over the edges.
7. Spoon the cooled mince filling into the pastry-lined pie dish, spreading it out evenly.
8. Sprinkle the grated cheese over the top of the mince filling.
9. Roll out the second sheet of puff pastry and place it over the top of the filling. Press the edges of the pastry together to seal, and trim any excess pastry.
10. Use a sharp knife to make a few small slits in the top of the pie to allow steam to escape during baking.
11. Optional: Beat an egg and brush it over the top of the pastry for a golden finish.
12. Bake the pie in the preheated oven for 25-30 minutes, or until the pastry is golden brown and cooked through.
13. Once baked, remove the pie from the oven and let it cool slightly before slicing and serving.

Enjoy your homemade mince and cheese pie as a delicious and satisfying meal, perfect for lunch or dinner!

Kiwi Lamb Chops

Ingredients:

- 8 lamb chops
- 2 tablespoons olive oil
- 2 cloves garlic, minced
- 1 tablespoon fresh rosemary, chopped (or 1 teaspoon dried rosemary)
- Salt and pepper, to taste
- Lemon wedges, for serving (optional)

Instructions:

1. Preheat your grill or barbecue to medium-high heat.
2. In a small bowl, mix together the olive oil, minced garlic, chopped rosemary, salt, and pepper to make a marinade.
3. Place the lamb chops in a shallow dish or resealable plastic bag, and pour the marinade over them. Make sure the chops are well coated with the marinade.
4. Allow the lamb chops to marinate for at least 30 minutes to 1 hour, or longer if time allows. This will help infuse them with flavor.
5. Once the lamb chops have finished marinating, remove them from the dish or bag and discard any excess marinade.
6. Place the lamb chops on the preheated grill or barbecue and cook for about 3-4 minutes on each side, or until they reach your desired level of doneness. For medium-rare, aim for an internal temperature of 63°C (145°F), while for medium, aim for 71°C (160°F).
7. Once cooked to your liking, remove the lamb chops from the grill and let them rest for a few minutes before serving. This allows the juices to redistribute and the meat to become tender.
8. Serve the kiwi lamb chops hot, accompanied by lemon wedges for squeezing over the top, if desired.

Enjoy your delicious kiwi lamb chops as a flavorful and satisfying main dish, perfect for any occasion! They pair well with roasted vegetables, salads, or your favorite side dishes.

Hāngī Pie

Ingredients:

For the Filling:

- 500g lamb shoulder or beef chuck, diced
- 2 onions, chopped
- 2 carrots, chopped
- 2 potatoes, chopped
- 1 cup frozen peas
- 2 cloves garlic, minced
- 2 tablespoons tomato paste
- 1 tablespoon Worcestershire sauce
- 1 teaspoon dried thyme
- Salt and pepper, to taste
- 2 cups beef or vegetable broth
- 2 tablespoons cooking oil

For the Pastry:

- 2 sheets of store-bought puff pastry, thawed
- 1 egg, beaten (for egg wash)

Instructions:

1. Preheat your oven to 200°C (400°F) and grease a pie dish or baking dish.
2. In a large skillet or frying pan, heat the cooking oil over medium-high heat. Add the diced lamb or beef and cook until browned on all sides. Remove the meat from the pan and set aside.
3. In the same pan, add the chopped onions and garlic. Cook until softened and fragrant, about 3-4 minutes.
4. Add the chopped carrots and potatoes to the pan and cook for another 5 minutes, stirring occasionally.
5. Return the cooked meat to the pan. Add the tomato paste, Worcestershire sauce, dried thyme, salt, and pepper. Stir to combine.

6. Pour in the beef or vegetable broth and bring the mixture to a simmer. Cover the pan and cook for about 30 minutes, or until the meat and vegetables are tender and the liquid has reduced to a thick gravy.
7. Stir in the frozen peas and cook for another 2-3 minutes, or until heated through. Remove the pan from the heat and let the filling cool slightly.
8. While the filling is cooling, prepare the pastry. Roll out one sheet of puff pastry and line the bottom of the greased pie dish with it. Trim any excess pastry hanging over the edges.
9. Spoon the cooled hangi filling into the pastry-lined pie dish, spreading it out evenly.
10. Roll out the second sheet of puff pastry and place it over the top of the filling. Press the edges of the pastry together to seal, and trim any excess pastry.
11. Use a sharp knife to make a few small slits in the top of the pie to allow steam to escape during baking.
12. Brush the beaten egg over the top of the pastry for a golden finish.
13. Bake the hangi pie in the preheated oven for 25-30 minutes, or until the pastry is golden brown and cooked through.
14. Once baked, remove the pie from the oven and let it cool slightly before slicing and serving.

Enjoy your homemade hangi pie as a delicious and hearty meal, perfect for lunch or dinner!

Kiwi Meatloaf

Ingredients:

- 500g ground beef or a mixture of beef and pork
- 1 onion, finely chopped
- 2 cloves garlic, minced
- 1 cup breadcrumbs
- 2 eggs
- 1/4 cup tomato sauce (ketchup)
- 2 tablespoons Worcestershire sauce
- 1 tablespoon mustard
- 1 teaspoon dried mixed herbs (such as thyme, rosemary, and oregano)
- Salt and pepper, to taste
- Cooking oil or cooking spray, for greasing

For the Glaze:

- 1/4 cup tomato sauce (ketchup)
- 1 tablespoon brown sugar
- 1 tablespoon Worcestershire sauce

Instructions:

1. Preheat your oven to 180°C (350°F) and grease a loaf pan with cooking oil or cooking spray.
2. In a large mixing bowl, combine the ground meat, chopped onion, minced garlic, breadcrumbs, eggs, tomato sauce, Worcestershire sauce, mustard, dried herbs, salt, and pepper. Use your hands or a spoon to mix everything together until well combined.
3. Transfer the meat mixture into the greased loaf pan, pressing it down firmly and smoothing the top with a spatula.
4. In a small bowl, mix together the ingredients for the glaze: tomato sauce, brown sugar, and Worcestershire sauce. Spread the glaze evenly over the top of the meatloaf.

5. Bake the meatloaf in the preheated oven for 45-55 minutes, or until cooked through and the top is caramelized and golden brown.
6. Once cooked, remove the meatloaf from the oven and let it rest in the loaf pan for 5-10 minutes before slicing.
7. Serve the kiwi meatloaf hot, sliced into thick slices, and accompanied by your favorite sides such as mashed potatoes, steamed vegetables, or a fresh salad.

Enjoy your homemade kiwi meatloaf as a comforting and satisfying meal, perfect for sharing with family and friends!

Seafood Chowder

Ingredients:

- 500g mixed seafood (such as shrimp, scallops, white fish, and/or mussels), peeled and deveined if necessary
- 2 tablespoons butter
- 1 onion, finely chopped
- 2 cloves garlic, minced
- 2 stalks celery, finely chopped
- 2 medium potatoes, peeled and diced
- 2 cups fish or seafood stock
- 1 cup milk or cream
- 1/4 cup all-purpose flour
- 1/2 cup frozen corn kernels
- 1/2 cup frozen peas
- 1 teaspoon dried thyme
- Salt and pepper, to taste
- Chopped fresh parsley, for garnish (optional)

Instructions:

1. In a large pot or Dutch oven, melt the butter over medium heat. Add the chopped onion and garlic, and sauté until softened and fragrant, about 3-4 minutes.
2. Add the chopped celery and diced potatoes to the pot, and cook for another 5 minutes, stirring occasionally.
3. Sprinkle the flour over the vegetables in the pot, and stir to coat them evenly. Cook for 1-2 minutes to remove the raw flour taste.
4. Gradually pour in the fish or seafood stock, stirring constantly to prevent lumps from forming. Bring the mixture to a simmer, and cook for about 10 minutes, or until the potatoes are tender and cooked through.
5. Add the mixed seafood, frozen corn kernels, frozen peas, and dried thyme to the pot. Simmer for another 5 minutes, or until the seafood is cooked through and opaque.
6. Pour in the milk or cream, and stir to combine. Season the chowder with salt and pepper to taste. Adjust the consistency by adding more milk or cream if desired.

7. Continue to simmer the chowder for another 5 minutes to heat through and allow the flavors to meld together.
8. Once the seafood chowder is ready, ladle it into bowls and garnish with chopped fresh parsley if desired.
9. Serve the seafood chowder hot, accompanied by crusty bread or oyster crackers.

Enjoy your homemade seafood chowder as a delicious and comforting meal, perfect for a chilly day!

Cheese Rolls

Ingredients:

- 8 slices of white bread
- 200g grated tasty cheese (cheddar or your preferred cheese)
- 1/4 cup evaporated milk
- 1/4 cup onion soup mix (optional)
- 50g butter, melted

Instructions:

1. Preheat your oven to 180°C (350°F) and line a baking sheet with parchment paper.
2. Trim the crusts from the slices of white bread.
3. In a mixing bowl, combine the grated cheese, evaporated milk, and onion soup mix (if using). Mix until well combined and the cheese is evenly coated.
4. Spread the cheese mixture evenly over each slice of bread.
5. Starting from one end, roll each slice of bread up tightly into a spiral.
6. Place the rolled-up cheese rolls seam-side down on the prepared baking sheet.
7. Brush the melted butter over the tops of the cheese rolls.
8. Bake the cheese rolls in the preheated oven for 15-20 minutes, or until golden brown and crispy.
9. Once baked, remove the cheese rolls from the oven and let them cool slightly before serving.
10. Serve the cheese rolls hot or warm as a delicious snack or appetizer.

Enjoy your homemade cheese rolls as a tasty and comforting treat! They're perfect for sharing with family and friends.

Māori Boil-Up

Ingredients:

- 500g pork bones or pork shoulder, chopped into pieces
- 1 onion, peeled and chopped
- 2 carrots, peeled and chopped into chunks
- 2 potatoes, peeled and chopped into chunks
- 1 kumara (sweet potato), peeled and chopped into chunks (optional)
- 2 cups chopped cabbage or other leafy greens (such as spinach or silverbeet)
- Salt and pepper, to taste
- Dumplings (optional)

Instructions:

1. In a large pot or Dutch oven, combine the pork bones or pork shoulder pieces with enough water to cover them. Bring the liquid to a boil over medium-high heat, then reduce the heat to low and simmer for about 1-2 hours, or until the pork is tender and cooked through. Skim off any foam or impurities that rise to the surface during cooking.
2. Once the pork is cooked, add the chopped onion, carrots, potatoes, and kumara (if using) to the pot. Simmer for another 15-20 minutes, or until the vegetables are tender.
3. Add the chopped cabbage or leafy greens to the pot and simmer for an additional 5-10 minutes, or until wilted.
4. Season the boil-up with salt and pepper to taste, adjusting the seasoning as needed.
5. If desired, add dumplings to the pot during the last 10-15 minutes of cooking. To make dumplings, simply mix together self-raising flour and enough water to form a stiff dough. Divide the dough into small balls and drop them into the simmering broth.
6. Once the vegetables are tender and the dumplings are cooked through, remove the pot from the heat.
7. Serve the Māori boil-up hot, ladled into bowls with plenty of the flavorful broth.

Enjoy this comforting and nourishing Māori dish as a delicious and satisfying meal, perfect for sharing with family and friends!

Bacon and Egg Pie

Ingredients:

- 6-8 slices of streaky bacon, chopped
- 6 large eggs
- 1/2 cup milk
- Salt and pepper, to taste
- 1 sheet of store-bought puff pastry, thawed
- 1/2 cup grated cheese (optional)
- Fresh herbs, such as chopped parsley or chives, for garnish (optional)

Instructions:

1. Preheat your oven to 200°C (400°F) and lightly grease a pie dish or baking dish.
2. In a frying pan, cook the chopped bacon over medium heat until crispy. Remove from the pan and drain on paper towels.
3. In a mixing bowl, whisk together the eggs and milk until well combined. Season with salt and pepper to taste.
4. Roll out the puff pastry sheet and line the greased pie dish with it, allowing any excess pastry to hang over the edges.
5. Sprinkle the cooked bacon evenly over the bottom of the pastry-lined pie dish.
6. Pour the egg mixture over the bacon, making sure it is evenly distributed.
7. If using grated cheese, sprinkle it over the top of the egg mixture.
8. Fold any excess pastry over the top of the filling, or trim it if preferred.
9. Bake the bacon and egg pie in the preheated oven for 25-30 minutes, or until the pastry is golden brown and the filling is set.
10. Once baked, remove the pie from the oven and let it cool slightly before slicing.
11. Garnish the bacon and egg pie with fresh herbs, if desired.
12. Serve the pie warm or at room temperature, either on its own or accompanied by a side salad or steamed vegetables.

Enjoy your homemade bacon and egg pie as a delicious and satisfying meal, perfect for any occasion!

Kiwi Dip

Ingredients:

- 1 cup sour cream (or cream cheese for a thicker consistency)
- 1/4 cup mayonnaise
- 1 tablespoon lemon juice
- 1 teaspoon onion soup mix (or finely chopped onion)
- 1 teaspoon Worcestershire sauce
- 1 teaspoon dried parsley
- 1/2 teaspoon garlic powder
- Salt and pepper, to taste
- Chopped fresh chives or green onions, for garnish (optional)

Instructions:

1. In a mixing bowl, combine the sour cream (or cream cheese) and mayonnaise.
2. Add the lemon juice, onion soup mix (or finely chopped onion), Worcestershire sauce, dried parsley, garlic powder, salt, and pepper to the bowl. Mix until all the ingredients are well combined.
3. Taste the dip and adjust the seasoning as needed, adding more salt, pepper, or other seasonings to suit your preference.
4. Transfer the kiwi dip to a serving bowl and garnish with chopped fresh chives or green onions, if desired.
5. Cover the bowl with plastic wrap and refrigerate the dip for at least 1 hour to allow the flavors to meld together.
6. Before serving, give the dip a quick stir and taste again to adjust the seasoning if necessary.
7. Serve the kiwi dip with a variety of dippable items such as chips, crackers, sliced vegetables, or breadsticks.

Enjoy your homemade kiwi dip as a tasty and versatile appetizer that's sure to be a hit at your next gathering or party! Feel free to customize the dip by adding other ingredients like grated cheese, bacon bits, or chopped herbs to suit your taste.

Kiwi Onion Dip

Ingredients:

- 2 large onions, thinly sliced
- 2 tablespoons butter
- 1 cup sour cream
- 1/2 cup mayonnaise
- 1 teaspoon garlic powder
- 1 teaspoon Worcestershire sauce
- Salt and pepper, to taste
- Chopped fresh chives or parsley, for garnish (optional)

Instructions:

1. In a large skillet or frying pan, melt the butter over medium heat. Add the thinly sliced onions and cook, stirring occasionally, until they are caramelized and golden brown, about 20-25 minutes. Be patient, as caramelizing the onions slowly over low heat will bring out their natural sweetness and flavor.
2. Once the onions are caramelized, remove them from the heat and let them cool slightly.
3. In a mixing bowl, combine the sour cream, mayonnaise, garlic powder, Worcestershire sauce, salt, and pepper. Stir until all the ingredients are well combined.
4. Add the caramelized onions to the sour cream mixture and stir until they are evenly distributed throughout the dip.
5. Taste the dip and adjust the seasoning as needed, adding more salt, pepper, or garlic powder to suit your preference.
6. Transfer the kiwi onion dip to a serving bowl and garnish with chopped fresh chives or parsley, if desired.
7. Cover the bowl with plastic wrap and refrigerate the dip for at least 1 hour to allow the flavors to meld together.
8. Before serving, give the dip a quick stir and taste again to adjust the seasoning if necessary.
9. Serve the kiwi onion dip with a variety of dippable items such as chips, crackers, sliced vegetables, or breadsticks.

Enjoy your homemade kiwi onion dip as a delicious and flavorful appetizer that's perfect for sharing with family and friends!

Kiwi Bacon and Egg Pie

Ingredients:

- 6-8 slices of streaky bacon, chopped
- 6 large eggs
- 1/4 cup milk
- Salt and pepper, to taste
- 1 sheet of store-bought puff pastry, thawed
- 1/2 cup grated cheese (optional)
- Fresh herbs, such as chopped parsley or chives, for garnish (optional)

Instructions:

1. Preheat your oven to 200°C (400°F) and lightly grease a pie dish or baking dish.
2. In a frying pan, cook the chopped bacon over medium heat until crispy. Remove from the pan and drain on paper towels.
3. In a mixing bowl, whisk together the eggs, milk, salt, and pepper until well combined.
4. Roll out the puff pastry sheet and line the greased pie dish with it, allowing any excess pastry to hang over the edges.
5. Sprinkle the cooked bacon evenly over the bottom of the pastry-lined pie dish.
6. Pour the egg mixture over the bacon, making sure it is evenly distributed.
7. If using grated cheese, sprinkle it over the top of the egg mixture.
8. Fold any excess pastry over the top of the filling, or trim it if preferred.
9. Bake the bacon and egg pie in the preheated oven for 25-30 minutes, or until the pastry is golden brown and the filling is set.
10. Once baked, remove the pie from the oven and let it cool slightly before slicing.
11. Garnish the bacon and egg pie with fresh herbs, if desired.
12. Serve the pie warm or at room temperature, either on its own or accompanied by a side salad or steamed vegetables.

Enjoy your homemade kiwi bacon and egg pie as a delicious and satisfying meal, perfect for any occasion!

Māori Fried Bread

Ingredients:

- 4 cups self-raising flour
- 1 teaspoon salt
- 1 tablespoon sugar
- 1 cup warm water (approximately)
- Oil for frying (such as canola or vegetable oil)

Instructions:

1. In a large mixing bowl, sift together the self-raising flour, salt, and sugar.
2. Gradually add warm water to the dry ingredients, stirring with a spoon or your hands to form a soft dough. Start with about 3/4 cup of water and add more as needed until the dough comes together. The dough should be soft and slightly sticky.
3. Turn the dough out onto a lightly floured surface and knead it for a few minutes until it becomes smooth and elastic.
4. Divide the dough into equal-sized portions, depending on how large you want your fried bread to be. Roll each portion into a ball and then flatten it slightly with your hands to form a disc or oval shape.
5. Heat oil in a large frying pan or skillet over medium heat. The oil should be hot but not smoking.
6. Carefully place the flattened dough discs into the hot oil, one or two at a time, depending on the size of your pan. Fry the bread for 2-3 minutes on each side, or until golden brown and cooked through. Use a spatula to flip the bread halfway through cooking.
7. Once cooked, remove the fried bread from the oil and place them on a plate lined with paper towels to drain any excess oil.
8. Repeat the frying process with the remaining dough portions, adding more oil to the pan as needed.
9. Serve the Māori fried bread hot, either plain or with your favorite toppings such as butter, jam, honey, or savory spreads.

Enjoy your delicious homemade Māori fried bread as a snack, side dish, or part of a meal!

Kiwi Sausage Rolls

Ingredients:

- 500g sausage meat (you can use pork, beef, or a mixture)
- 1 onion, finely chopped
- 2 cloves garlic, minced
- 1 carrot, grated
- 1 tablespoon tomato sauce (ketchup)
- 1 tablespoon Worcestershire sauce
- 1 teaspoon dried mixed herbs (such as thyme, rosemary, and oregano)
- Salt and pepper, to taste
- 2 sheets of store-bought puff pastry, thawed
- 1 egg, beaten (for egg wash)
- Sesame seeds or poppy seeds (optional, for garnish)

Instructions:

1. Preheat your oven to 200°C (400°F) and line a baking sheet with parchment paper.
2. In a mixing bowl, combine the sausage meat, chopped onion, minced garlic, grated carrot, tomato sauce, Worcestershire sauce, dried herbs, salt, and pepper. Mix until all the ingredients are well combined.
3. Roll out one sheet of puff pastry on a lightly floured surface. Cut the pastry in half lengthwise to make two long rectangles.
4. Divide the sausage meat mixture into two equal portions. Shape each portion into a long log and place it down the center of each pastry rectangle.
5. Brush one edge of the pastry with beaten egg. Roll the pastry over the sausage meat to enclose it, pressing the edges to seal. Repeat with the other pastry rectangle.
6. Cut each long sausage roll into smaller pieces, about 5-6 cm (2-2.5 inches) long.
7. Place the sausage rolls on the prepared baking sheet, seam-side down. Brush the tops with beaten egg and sprinkle with sesame seeds or poppy seeds, if using.
8. Bake the sausage rolls in the preheated oven for 20-25 minutes, or until the pastry is golden brown and crispy, and the sausage meat is cooked through.
9. Once baked, remove the sausage rolls from the oven and let them cool slightly before serving.

10. Serve the kiwi sausage rolls warm as a delicious snack or appetizer, accompanied by your favorite dipping sauce or chutney.

Enjoy your homemade kiwi sausage rolls as a tasty and satisfying treat! They're perfect for parties, picnics, or any occasion.

Kiwi Potato Salad

Ingredients:

- 1 kg potatoes (choose waxy varieties like new potatoes or red potatoes)
- 3 eggs
- 1/2 cup mayonnaise
- 2 tablespoons plain Greek yogurt (optional, for added creaminess)
- 2 tablespoons whole grain mustard
- 1 tablespoon apple cider vinegar
- 1/2 cup chopped celery
- 1/4 cup chopped red onion
- 2 tablespoons chopped fresh parsley (or chives)
- Salt and pepper, to taste
- Paprika, for garnish (optional)

Instructions:

1. Start by boiling the potatoes: Wash the potatoes and cut them into bite-sized chunks. Place them in a large pot of salted water and bring to a boil. Cook until the potatoes are tender when pierced with a fork, about 10-15 minutes. Drain the potatoes and let them cool slightly.
2. While the potatoes are cooking, place the eggs in a separate pot and cover them with cold water. Bring the water to a boil, then remove the pot from the heat, cover, and let the eggs sit in the hot water for 10-12 minutes. Drain the hot water, then transfer the eggs to a bowl of ice water to cool. Once cooled, peel the eggs and chop them into small pieces.
3. In a large mixing bowl, combine the mayonnaise, Greek yogurt (if using), whole grain mustard, and apple cider vinegar. Stir until well combined and smooth.
4. Add the chopped celery, red onion, and chopped parsley (or chives) to the bowl with the dressing. Mix well to combine.
5. Once the potatoes are cooled slightly, add them to the bowl with the dressing and vegetables. Gently toss until the potatoes are evenly coated with the dressing.
6. Fold in the chopped hard-boiled eggs, being careful not to break them up too much.
7. Taste the potato salad and season with salt and pepper to taste. Adjust the seasoning as needed.

8. Transfer the potato salad to a serving dish and sprinkle with paprika for garnish, if desired.
9. Cover the potato salad and refrigerate for at least 1 hour before serving to allow the flavors to meld together.
10. Serve the kiwi potato salad chilled or at room temperature as a delicious side dish to accompany grilled meats, sandwiches, or other summer favorites.

Enjoy your homemade kiwi potato salad as a tasty and refreshing addition to your next meal or gathering!

Green-Lipped Mussel Soup

Ingredients:

- 500g green-lipped mussels, cleaned and debearded
- 2 tablespoons butter or olive oil
- 1 onion, finely chopped
- 2 cloves garlic, minced
- 1 carrot, diced
- 1 celery stalk, diced
- 1 potato, diced
- 4 cups fish or vegetable broth
- 1 cup coconut milk
- 1 teaspoon curry powder
- Salt and pepper, to taste
- Fresh cilantro or parsley, for garnish

Instructions:

1. Heat the butter or olive oil in a large pot over medium heat. Add the chopped onion and minced garlic, and sauté until softened and fragrant, about 3-4 minutes.
2. Add the diced carrot, celery, and potato to the pot, and cook for another 5 minutes, stirring occasionally.
3. Pour the fish or vegetable broth into the pot and bring the mixture to a simmer. Cook for about 10-15 minutes, or until the vegetables are tender.
4. While the soup is simmering, prepare the green-lipped mussels. Rinse them thoroughly under cold water and debeard them if necessary.
5. Add the cleaned mussels to the pot and cook for 5-7 minutes, or until they have opened up. Discard any mussels that do not open.
6. Stir in the coconut milk and curry powder, and season the soup with salt and pepper to taste. Simmer for another 5 minutes to allow the flavors to meld together.
7. Once the soup is ready, ladle it into bowls and garnish with fresh cilantro or parsley.
8. Serve the green-lipped mussel soup hot, accompanied by crusty bread or crackers.

Enjoy your homemade green-lipped mussel soup as a delicious and comforting meal, packed with the flavors of New Zealand's coastal waters!

Kiwi Crayfish Salad

Ingredients:

- 2 cooked crayfish (also known as rock lobsters), meat removed from the shell and chopped into bite-sized pieces
- 1 avocado, diced
- 1 mango, diced
- 1/2 red onion, finely chopped
- 1/2 cucumber, diced
- 1 red bell pepper, diced
- Juice of 1 lime
- 2 tablespoons chopped fresh cilantro (coriander)
- Salt and pepper, to taste
- Mixed salad greens, for serving

Instructions:

1. In a large mixing bowl, combine the chopped crayfish meat, diced avocado, diced mango, chopped red onion, diced cucumber, and diced red bell pepper.
2. Squeeze the lime juice over the salad ingredients and add the chopped fresh cilantro. Season with salt and pepper to taste.
3. Gently toss the salad ingredients until everything is well combined and evenly coated with the lime juice and cilantro.
4. To serve, arrange a bed of mixed salad greens on individual plates or a large serving platter.
5. Spoon the crayfish salad mixture over the bed of salad greens, distributing it evenly.
6. Garnish the salad with additional chopped cilantro if desired.
7. Serve the kiwi crayfish salad immediately as a light and refreshing appetizer or main course.

Enjoy your homemade kiwi crayfish salad, a delightful dish that captures the flavors of New Zealand's coastal cuisine!

Kiwi Garlic Prawns

Ingredients:

- 500g large prawns, peeled and deveined
- 4 cloves garlic, minced
- 2 tablespoons butter
- 2 tablespoons olive oil
- Juice of 1 lemon
- 2 tablespoons chopped fresh parsley
- Salt and pepper, to taste
- Lemon wedges, for serving
- Crusty bread, for serving (optional)

Instructions:

1. In a large skillet or frying pan, heat the butter and olive oil over medium heat until the butter is melted and the oil is hot.
2. Add the minced garlic to the skillet and cook for 1-2 minutes, stirring frequently, until fragrant.
3. Add the peeled and deveined prawns to the skillet, spreading them out in a single layer. Cook for 2-3 minutes on one side, until they start to turn pink.
4. Flip the prawns over and cook for another 2-3 minutes on the other side, until they are cooked through and opaque.
5. Squeeze the lemon juice over the prawns and sprinkle them with chopped fresh parsley. Season with salt and pepper to taste.
6. Toss the prawns in the garlic butter sauce to coat them evenly.
7. Once the prawns are cooked and coated with the garlic butter sauce, remove the skillet from the heat.
8. Serve the kiwi garlic prawns hot, garnished with lemon wedges for squeezing over the top. Serve with crusty bread on the side for dipping into the flavorful sauce, if desired.

Enjoy your homemade kiwi garlic prawns as a delicious appetizer or main course, perfect for sharing with family and friends!

Kiwi Salmon Pie

Ingredients:

- 500g large prawns, peeled and deveined
- 4 cloves garlic, minced
- 2 tablespoons butter
- 2 tablespoons olive oil
- Juice of 1 lemon
- 2 tablespoons chopped fresh parsley
- Salt and pepper, to taste
- Lemon wedges, for serving
- Crusty bread, for serving (optional)

Instructions:

1. In a large skillet or frying pan, heat the butter and olive oil over medium heat until the butter is melted and the oil is hot.
2. Add the minced garlic to the skillet and cook for 1-2 minutes, stirring frequently, until fragrant.
3. Add the peeled and deveined prawns to the skillet, spreading them out in a single layer. Cook for 2-3 minutes on one side, until they start to turn pink.
4. Flip the prawns over and cook for another 2-3 minutes on the other side, until they are cooked through and opaque.
5. Squeeze the lemon juice over the prawns and sprinkle them with chopped fresh parsley. Season with salt and pepper to taste.
6. Toss the prawns in the garlic butter sauce to coat them evenly.
7. Once the prawns are cooked and coated with the garlic butter sauce, remove the skillet from the heat.
8. Serve the kiwi garlic prawns hot, garnished with lemon wedges for squeezing over the top. Serve with crusty bread on the side for dipping into the flavorful sauce, if desired.

Enjoy your homemade kiwi garlic prawns as a delicious appetizer or main course, perfect for sharing with family and friends!

Kiwi Salmon Pie

Ingredients:

- 500g fresh salmon fillets, skin removed and cut into bite-sized pieces
- 1 onion, finely chopped
- 2 cloves garlic, minced
- 1 carrot, diced
- 1 celery stalk, diced
- 2 tablespoons butter
- 2 tablespoons all-purpose flour
- 1 cup milk
- 1 cup fish or vegetable broth
- 1/2 cup frozen peas
- 2 tablespoons chopped fresh parsley
- Salt and pepper, to taste
- 2 sheets of store-bought puff pastry, thawed
- 1 egg, beaten (for egg wash)

Instructions:

1. Preheat your oven to 200°C (400°F) and lightly grease a pie dish or baking dish.
2. In a large skillet or frying pan, melt the butter over medium heat. Add the chopped onion and minced garlic, and sauté until softened and fragrant, about 3-4 minutes.
3. Add the diced carrot and celery to the skillet, and cook for another 5 minutes, stirring occasionally.
4. Stir in the all-purpose flour and cook for 1-2 minutes to create a roux.
5. Gradually add the milk and fish or vegetable broth to the skillet, stirring constantly to prevent lumps from forming. Cook until the mixture thickens and becomes creamy.
6. Add the bite-sized salmon pieces to the skillet, along with the frozen peas and chopped fresh parsley. Season with salt and pepper to taste. Cook for another 3-4 minutes, or until the salmon is cooked through and the peas are heated through.
7. Remove the skillet from the heat and let the filling cool slightly.

8. Roll out one sheet of puff pastry on a lightly floured surface and line the greased pie dish with it, allowing any excess pastry to hang over the edges.
9. Spoon the salmon filling into the pastry-lined pie dish, spreading it out evenly.
10. Roll out the remaining sheet of puff pastry and place it over the top of the filling. Trim any excess pastry and crimp the edges to seal the pie.
11. Brush the top of the pie with beaten egg to create a golden crust.
12. Use a sharp knife to make a few small slits in the top of the pastry to allow steam to escape during baking.
13. Bake the salmon pie in the preheated oven for 25-30 minutes, or until the pastry is golden brown and crispy.
14. Once baked, remove the pie from the oven and let it cool slightly before slicing and serving.

Enjoy your homemade kiwi salmon pie as a delicious and satisfying meal, perfect for any occasion!

Kiwi Venison Stew

Ingredients:

- 500g venison stew meat, cubed
- 2 tablespoons olive oil
- 1 onion, chopped
- 2 cloves garlic, minced
- 2 carrots, peeled and chopped
- 2 celery stalks, chopped
- 2 potatoes, peeled and chopped
- 2 cups beef or venison broth
- 1 cup red wine (optional)
- 2 tablespoons tomato paste
- 1 teaspoon dried thyme
- 1 teaspoon dried rosemary
- Salt and pepper, to taste
- Chopped fresh parsley, for garnish (optional)

Instructions:

1. In a large pot or Dutch oven, heat the olive oil over medium heat. Add the cubed venison meat to the pot and cook until browned on all sides, about 5-7 minutes. Remove the meat from the pot and set aside.
2. In the same pot, add the chopped onion and minced garlic. Cook until softened and fragrant, about 3-4 minutes.
3. Add the chopped carrots, celery, and potatoes to the pot, and cook for another 5 minutes, stirring occasionally.
4. Return the browned venison meat to the pot. Pour in the beef or venison broth and red wine (if using), stirring to deglaze the bottom of the pot.
5. Stir in the tomato paste, dried thyme, dried rosemary, salt, and pepper.
6. Bring the stew to a simmer, then reduce the heat to low and cover the pot with a lid. Let the stew simmer gently for 1.5 to 2 hours, or until the venison is tender and the vegetables are cooked through.
7. Taste the stew and adjust the seasoning as needed, adding more salt and pepper if desired.

8. Once the stew is cooked to your liking, remove it from the heat and let it rest for a few minutes before serving.
9. Serve the kiwi venison stew hot, garnished with chopped fresh parsley if desired.

Enjoy your homemade kiwi venison stew as a comforting and satisfying meal, perfect for cooler days or special occasions!

Kiwi Fish and Chips

Ingredients:

For the fish:

- 4 fillets of firm white fish (such as hoki, snapper, or tarakihi)
- 1 cup all-purpose flour
- 1 teaspoon baking powder
- 1 teaspoon salt
- 1 cup beer (use your favorite lager or ale)

For the chips:

- 4 large potatoes (suitable for frying, such as Agria or Russet)
- Vegetable oil, for frying
- Salt, to taste

For serving:

- Lemon wedges
- Malt vinegar
- Tartar sauce or aioli (optional)

Instructions:

1. Start by preparing the fish. In a mixing bowl, whisk together the flour, baking powder, and salt. Gradually add the beer, stirring until you have a smooth batter. Let the batter rest for 15-20 minutes while you prepare the chips.
2. Peel the potatoes and cut them into thick chips or wedges. Rinse them under cold water to remove excess starch, then pat them dry with paper towels.
3. Heat vegetable oil in a deep fryer or large pot to 180°C (350°F). Fry the potato chips in batches until they are golden brown and crispy, about 5-7 minutes per

batch. Remove them from the oil using a slotted spoon and drain on paper towels. Sprinkle with salt while they are still hot.
4. While the chips are frying, dip each fish fillet into the batter, coating it evenly. Carefully place the battered fish into the hot oil and fry until golden brown and cooked through, about 4-5 minutes per side. Remove the fish from the oil and drain on paper towels.
5. Serve the fish and chips hot, with lemon wedges, malt vinegar, and tartar sauce or aioli on the side.

Enjoy your homemade kiwi fish and chips as a delicious and satisfying meal, reminiscent of the classic takeaway dish enjoyed throughout New Zealand!

Kiwi Hangi Parcels

Ingredients:

- 500g lamb or chicken, diced
- 2 cups kumara (sweet potato), peeled and diced
- 2 cups pumpkin, peeled and diced
- 2 cups potatoes, peeled and diced
- 2 cups carrots, peeled and diced
- 1 onion, diced
- 2 cloves garlic, minced
- 2 tablespoons olive oil
- Salt and pepper, to taste
- 1 tablespoon dried mixed herbs (such as thyme, rosemary, and oregano)
- Aluminum foil

Instructions:

1. Preheat your oven to 200°C (400°F) and prepare large sheets of aluminum foil for wrapping the parcels.
2. In a large mixing bowl, combine the diced lamb or chicken, diced kumara, pumpkin, potatoes, carrots, diced onion, and minced garlic.
3. Drizzle the olive oil over the mixture and sprinkle with salt, pepper, and dried mixed herbs. Toss everything together until well coated.
4. Divide the mixture into portions and place each portion onto a sheet of aluminum foil.
5. Fold the aluminum foil over the mixture to form a parcel, sealing the edges tightly to prevent any steam from escaping during cooking.
6. Place the parcels on a baking sheet and bake in the preheated oven for 45-60 minutes, or until the meat is cooked through and the vegetables are tender.
7. Carefully open the parcels and transfer the contents to serving plates.
8. Serve the kiwi hangi parcels hot, accompanied by your favorite sauce or condiments, such as mint sauce or tomato relish.

Enjoy your homemade kiwi hangi parcels as a delicious and flavorful meal, reminiscent of the traditional Māori hangi cooking method!

Kiwi Roast Lamb

Ingredients:

- 1 leg of lamb (around 2-2.5kg), bone-in or boneless
- 4 cloves garlic, thinly sliced
- 2 tablespoons fresh rosemary leaves, chopped (or 1 tablespoon dried rosemary)
- 2 tablespoons fresh thyme leaves, chopped (or 1 tablespoon dried thyme)
- 2 tablespoons olive oil
- Salt and pepper, to taste
- 1 cup beef or vegetable broth (or water)

Instructions:

1. Preheat your oven to 180°C (350°F).
2. Using a sharp knife, make small incisions all over the surface of the lamb leg. Insert the garlic slices into the incisions.
3. In a small bowl, combine the chopped rosemary, thyme, olive oil, salt, and pepper to make a herb paste.
4. Rub the herb paste all over the surface of the lamb leg, making sure to coat it evenly.
5. Place the lamb leg in a roasting pan, fat side up. Pour the broth or water into the bottom of the roasting pan.
6. Cover the roasting pan with aluminum foil and roast the lamb in the preheated oven for about 1 hour.
7. After 1 hour, remove the aluminum foil and continue roasting the lamb for another 1 to 1.5 hours, or until the internal temperature reaches your desired level of doneness. For medium-rare, the internal temperature should be around 55-60°C (130-140°F) when measured with a meat thermometer inserted into the thickest part of the meat.
8. Once the lamb is cooked to your liking, remove it from the oven and let it rest for 10-15 minutes before carving.
9. Carve the roast lamb into slices and serve hot, accompanied by your favorite sides such as roasted vegetables, mashed potatoes, or a fresh salad.

Enjoy your homemade kiwi roast lamb as a delicious and comforting meal, perfect for sharing with family and friends!

Kiwi Lamb Shank Soup

Ingredients:

- 4 lamb shanks
- 2 tablespoons olive oil
- 1 onion, chopped
- 2 carrots, chopped
- 2 celery stalks, chopped
- 2 cloves garlic, minced
- 2 bay leaves
- 1 teaspoon dried thyme
- 1 teaspoon dried rosemary
- 1/2 cup red wine (optional)
- 6 cups beef or vegetable broth
- 2 cups water
- 2 large potatoes, peeled and diced
- Salt and pepper, to taste
- Chopped fresh parsley, for garnish

Instructions:

1. Preheat your oven to 180°C (350°F).
2. Heat the olive oil in a large oven-safe pot or Dutch oven over medium-high heat. Season the lamb shanks with salt and pepper, then add them to the pot. Sear the lamb shanks until browned on all sides, about 3-4 minutes per side. Remove the lamb shanks from the pot and set aside.
3. Add the chopped onion, carrots, and celery to the pot. Cook, stirring occasionally, until the vegetables are softened, about 5 minutes. Add the minced garlic, bay leaves, dried thyme, and dried rosemary, and cook for another 1-2 minutes until fragrant.
4. If using red wine, pour it into the pot and stir, scraping up any browned bits from the bottom of the pot.
5. Return the lamb shanks to the pot and pour in the beef or vegetable broth and water. Bring the liquid to a simmer.
6. Cover the pot with a lid and transfer it to the preheated oven. Let the soup cook in the oven for 2-3 hours, or until the lamb is tender and falling off the bone.

7. Remove the pot from the oven and carefully transfer the lamb shanks to a plate. Use a fork to shred the meat from the bones, then return the meat to the pot.
8. Add the diced potatoes to the pot and simmer the soup on the stovetop until the potatoes are tender, about 20-30 minutes.
9. Taste the soup and adjust the seasoning with salt and pepper as needed.
10. Serve the kiwi lamb shank soup hot, garnished with chopped fresh parsley.

Enjoy your homemade kiwi lamb shank soup as a comforting and satisfying meal!

Kiwi Mussel Soup

Ingredients:

- 1 kg fresh green-lipped mussels, cleaned and debearded
- 2 tablespoons butter or olive oil
- 1 onion, finely chopped
- 2 cloves garlic, minced
- 1 celery stalk, diced
- 1 carrot, diced
- 2 potatoes, peeled and diced
- 4 cups fish or vegetable broth
- 1 cup white wine (optional)
- 1 cup heavy cream (or coconut milk for a dairy-free option)
- Salt and pepper, to taste
- Chopped fresh parsley or chives, for garnish
- Lemon wedges, for serving

Instructions:

1. Start by cleaning the mussels. Rinse them under cold water, scrubbing off any debris or grit. Remove the beards by pulling them firmly towards the hinged end of the shell. Discard any mussels that are open or do not close when tapped.
2. In a large pot or Dutch oven, heat the butter or olive oil over medium heat. Add the chopped onion and minced garlic, and sauté until softened and fragrant, about 3-4 minutes.
3. Add the diced celery, carrot, and potatoes to the pot, and cook for another 5 minutes, stirring occasionally.
4. Pour in the fish or vegetable broth and white wine (if using), and bring the mixture to a simmer.
5. Add the cleaned mussels to the pot and cover with a lid. Let the mussels steam for about 5-7 minutes, or until they have opened up. Discard any mussels that do not open.
6. Once the mussels are cooked, remove them from the pot with a slotted spoon and set them aside. Leave the broth mixture in the pot.

7. Use an immersion blender to puree the broth mixture until smooth. Alternatively, you can transfer the mixture to a blender and blend until smooth, then return it to the pot.
8. Stir in the heavy cream (or coconut milk) and season the soup with salt and pepper to taste.
9. Ladle the soup into bowls and top with the cooked mussels.
10. Garnish the kiwi mussel soup with chopped fresh parsley or chives, and serve with lemon wedges on the side for squeezing over the mussels.

Enjoy your homemade kiwi mussel soup as a flavorful and satisfying meal, perfect for showcasing New Zealand's delicious seafood!

Kiwi Smoked Fish Pie

Ingredients:

- 500g smoked fish fillets (such as haddock, mackerel, or trout), flaked
- 2 tablespoons butter
- 1 onion, finely chopped
- 2 cloves garlic, minced
- 2 tablespoons all-purpose flour
- 1 1/2 cups milk
- 1/2 cup fish or vegetable broth
- 1 cup frozen peas
- 2 tablespoons chopped fresh parsley
- Salt and pepper, to taste
- 1 sheet store-bought puff pastry, thawed
- 1 egg, beaten (for egg wash)

Instructions:

1. Preheat your oven to 200°C (400°F).
2. In a large skillet or frying pan, melt the butter over medium heat. Add the chopped onion and minced garlic, and sauté until softened and fragrant, about 3-4 minutes.
3. Stir in the all-purpose flour and cook for 1-2 minutes to create a roux.
4. Gradually pour in the milk and fish or vegetable broth, stirring constantly to prevent lumps from forming. Cook until the sauce thickens and becomes smooth.
5. Add the flaked smoked fish, frozen peas, and chopped fresh parsley to the skillet. Season with salt and pepper to taste. Stir until all ingredients are well combined and heated through. Remove from heat.
6. Transfer the fish mixture to a baking dish or pie dish, spreading it out evenly.
7. Roll out the puff pastry sheet on a lightly floured surface to fit the size of your baking dish. Place the pastry over the fish mixture, trimming any excess pastry from the edges.
8. Use a sharp knife to make a few small slits in the top of the pastry to allow steam to escape during baking.
9. Brush the pastry with beaten egg to create a golden crust.

10. Bake the smoked fish pie in the preheated oven for 25-30 minutes, or until the pastry is golden brown and crispy.
11. Once baked, remove the pie from the oven and let it cool slightly before serving.
12. Serve the kiwi smoked fish pie hot, accompanied by your favorite side dishes such as mashed potatoes and steamed vegetables.

Enjoy your homemade kiwi smoked fish pie as a delicious and comforting meal, perfect for any occasion!

Kiwi Spaghetti on Toast

Ingredients:

- 200g spaghetti
- 1 tablespoon butter
- 1 tablespoon all-purpose flour
- 1 cup milk
- Salt and pepper, to taste
- Grated cheese, for topping (optional)
- Chopped fresh parsley, for garnish (optional)
- Slices of toast, to serve

Instructions:

1. Cook the spaghetti according to the package instructions until al dente. Drain and set aside.
2. In a saucepan, melt the butter over medium heat. Once melted, add the flour and whisk constantly for about 1 minute to make a roux.
3. Gradually pour in the milk while whisking continuously to avoid lumps. Cook the mixture until it thickens and becomes smooth, about 3-5 minutes.
4. Season the white sauce with salt and pepper to taste. You can also add a pinch of nutmeg for extra flavor if desired.
5. Add the cooked spaghetti to the white sauce and toss until the spaghetti is well coated.
6. Toast slices of bread until golden brown and crispy.
7. Serve the spaghetti on top of the toast slices. If desired, sprinkle grated cheese over the spaghetti and toast.
8. Garnish with chopped fresh parsley for a pop of color and added freshness.
9. Serve the kiwi spaghetti on toast hot and enjoy!

This dish is versatile, and you can customize it according to your preferences. Some people like to add cooked bacon or chopped tomatoes to the spaghetti for extra flavor. Feel free to experiment and make it your own!

Kiwi Muttonbird Pie

Ingredients:

- 500g cooked muttonbird meat, shredded
- 1 onion, finely chopped
- 2 cloves garlic, minced
- 2 carrots, diced
- 2 celery stalks, diced
- 2 tablespoons butter or olive oil
- 2 tablespoons all-purpose flour
- 2 cups chicken or vegetable broth
- 1 cup milk or cream
- Salt and pepper, to taste
- 1 sheet store-bought puff pastry, thawed
- 1 egg, beaten (for egg wash)

Instructions:

1. Preheat your oven to 200°C (400°F).
2. In a large skillet or frying pan, heat the butter or olive oil over medium heat. Add the chopped onion and minced garlic, and sauté until softened and fragrant, about 3-4 minutes.
3. Add the diced carrots and celery to the skillet, and cook for another 5 minutes, stirring occasionally.
4. Sprinkle the flour over the vegetables in the skillet and stir to combine. Cook for 1-2 minutes to cook out the raw taste of the flour.
5. Gradually pour in the chicken or vegetable broth and milk or cream, stirring constantly to prevent lumps from forming. Cook until the mixture thickens and becomes smooth.
6. Add the shredded muttonbird meat to the skillet and stir until well combined. Season with salt and pepper to taste.
7. Transfer the muttonbird mixture to a baking dish.
8. Roll out the puff pastry sheet on a lightly floured surface to fit the size of your baking dish. Place the pastry over the muttonbird mixture, trimming any excess pastry from the edges.

9. Use a sharp knife to make a few small slits in the top of the pastry to allow steam to escape during baking.
10. Brush the pastry with beaten egg to create a golden crust.
11. Bake the muttonbird pie in the preheated oven for 25-30 minutes, or until the pastry is golden brown and crispy.
12. Once baked, remove the pie from the oven and let it cool slightly before serving.

Enjoy your homemade kiwi muttonbird pie as a unique and flavorful dish, perfect for sharing with friends and family!

Kiwi Roast Beef

Ingredients:

- 1.5 to 2 kg beef roast (such as topside, sirloin, or ribeye)
- 2 tablespoons olive oil
- 2 cloves garlic, minced
- 1 tablespoon Worcestershire sauce
- 1 tablespoon Dijon mustard
- 1 teaspoon dried thyme
- 1 teaspoon dried rosemary
- Salt and pepper, to taste
- Vegetables for roasting (such as potatoes, carrots, and onions)
- Beef stock or water, for basting

Instructions:

1. Preheat your oven to 180°C (350°F).
2. In a small bowl, combine the olive oil, minced garlic, Worcestershire sauce, Dijon mustard, dried thyme, dried rosemary, salt, and pepper to create a marinade.
3. Place the beef roast in a large roasting pan or baking dish. Rub the marinade all over the surface of the roast, ensuring it is evenly coated. Let the roast marinate for at least 30 minutes, or ideally overnight in the refrigerator for maximum flavor.
4. Arrange the vegetables around the beef roast in the roasting pan. You can cut the vegetables into large chunks and toss them with a little olive oil, salt, and pepper before placing them in the pan.
5. Place the roasting pan in the preheated oven and roast the beef for about 20 minutes per 500g for medium-rare doneness, or adjust the cooking time according to your preferred level of doneness. Use a meat thermometer inserted into the thickest part of the roast to check the internal temperature. For medium-rare, the temperature should register around 55-60°C (130-140°F).
6. Baste the beef roast with beef stock or water every 30 minutes or so to keep it moist and flavorful.
7. Once the beef roast reaches your desired level of doneness, remove it from the oven and transfer it to a carving board. Cover the roast loosely with aluminum foil and let it rest for 15-20 minutes before slicing. This allows the juices to redistribute throughout the meat, resulting in a juicier and more tender roast.

8. Carve the roast beef into thin slices and serve hot, accompanied by the roasted vegetables and your favorite gravy or sauce.

Enjoy your homemade kiwi roast beef as a delicious and satisfying meal, perfect for any occasion!

Kiwi Roast Chicken

Ingredients:

- 1 whole chicken (about 1.5 to 2 kg)
- 2 tablespoons butter, softened
- 2 cloves garlic, minced
- 1 tablespoon fresh herbs (such as thyme, rosemary, or parsley), chopped
- 1 lemon, halved
- Salt and pepper, to taste
- Vegetables for roasting (such as potatoes, carrots, and onions)

Instructions:

1. Preheat your oven to 200°C (400°F).
2. Remove any giblets from the cavity of the chicken and pat the chicken dry with paper towels.
3. In a small bowl, mix together the softened butter, minced garlic, chopped fresh herbs, salt, and pepper.
4. Rub the butter mixture all over the surface of the chicken, making sure to coat it evenly. You can also gently loosen the skin of the chicken and rub some of the butter mixture underneath the skin for extra flavor.
5. Place the halved lemon inside the cavity of the chicken. This will help to infuse the chicken with flavor and keep it moist during roasting.
6. Truss the chicken, if desired, by tying the legs together with kitchen twine. This helps the chicken cook more evenly and retains its shape.
7. Place the chicken in a roasting pan or baking dish, breast side up.
8. Arrange the vegetables around the chicken in the roasting pan. You can cut the vegetables into large chunks and toss them with a little olive oil, salt, and pepper before placing them in the pan.
9. Roast the chicken in the preheated oven for about 20 minutes per 500g, or until the internal temperature reaches 75°C (165°F) when measured with a meat thermometer inserted into the thickest part of the chicken.
10. Once the chicken is cooked through and golden brown, remove it from the oven and let it rest for 10-15 minutes before carving.
11. Carve the roast chicken into serving portions and serve hot, accompanied by the roasted vegetables.

Enjoy your homemade kiwi roast chicken as a delicious and comforting meal, perfect for sharing with family and friends!

Kiwi Bacon-Wrapped Sausages

Ingredients:

- 8-10 pork sausages (any variety you prefer)
- 8-10 rashers of streaky bacon
- Toothpicks or wooden skewers

Instructions:

1. Preheat your oven to 200°C (400°F) and line a baking sheet with parchment paper or aluminum foil.
2. Take each sausage and wrap it with a rasher of streaky bacon. You can stretch the bacon slightly if needed to ensure it covers the sausage completely.
3. Secure the bacon in place by inserting toothpicks or wooden skewers through the ends of the bacon and into the sausage. This will prevent the bacon from unraveling during cooking.
4. Place the bacon-wrapped sausages on the prepared baking sheet, leaving a little space between each one.
5. Bake the sausages in the preheated oven for 20-25 minutes, or until the bacon is crispy and golden brown, and the sausages are cooked through.
6. Once cooked, remove the sausages from the oven and let them cool slightly before serving.
7. Serve the kiwi bacon-wrapped sausages hot, either on their own as a snack or appetizer, or as part of a larger meal. They pair well with sauces like tomato relish or barbecue sauce for dipping.

Enjoy your homemade kiwi bacon-wrapped sausages as a delicious and satisfying treat!

Kiwi Fish Pie

Ingredients:

- 500g firm white fish fillets (such as haddock, cod, or snapper), cut into bite-sized pieces
- 200g smoked fish (such as haddock or mackerel), flaked
- 2 tablespoons butter
- 1 onion, finely chopped
- 2 cloves garlic, minced
- 2 carrots, diced
- 2 celery stalks, diced
- 2 tablespoons all-purpose flour
- 1 1/2 cups fish or vegetable broth
- 1 cup milk or cream
- 1 cup frozen peas
- 2 tablespoons chopped fresh parsley
- Salt and pepper, to taste
- 4-5 large potatoes, peeled and chopped
- 2 tablespoons butter
- 1/4 cup milk or cream
- Salt and pepper, to taste
- Grated cheese, for topping (optional)

Instructions:

1. Preheat your oven to 180°C (350°F).
2. In a large skillet or frying pan, melt the butter over medium heat. Add the chopped onion and minced garlic, and sauté until softened and fragrant, about 3-4 minutes.
3. Add the diced carrots and celery to the skillet, and cook for another 5 minutes, stirring occasionally.
4. Stir in the all-purpose flour and cook for 1-2 minutes to create a roux.
5. Gradually pour in the fish or vegetable broth and milk or cream, stirring constantly to prevent lumps from forming. Cook until the mixture thickens and becomes smooth.

6. Add the bite-sized white fish pieces, flaked smoked fish, frozen peas, and chopped fresh parsley to the skillet. Season with salt and pepper to taste. Cook for another 3-4 minutes, or until the fish is cooked through and the peas are heated through.
7. Meanwhile, cook the chopped potatoes in boiling salted water until tender. Drain well, then mash the potatoes with butter, milk or cream, salt, and pepper until smooth and creamy.
8. Transfer the fish mixture to a baking dish. Spread the mashed potatoes evenly over the top of the fish mixture.
9. If desired, sprinkle grated cheese over the mashed potatoes for an extra cheesy topping.
10. Bake the fish pie in the preheated oven for 25-30 minutes, or until the top is golden brown and the filling is bubbling.
11. Once baked, remove the pie from the oven and let it cool slightly before serving.
12. Serve the kiwi fish pie hot, accompanied by your favorite side dishes such as steamed vegetables or a fresh salad.

Enjoy your homemade kiwi fish pie as a delicious and comforting meal!

Kiwi Beef Stew

Ingredients:

- 1 kg beef chuck or stewing beef, cut into bite-sized pieces
- 2 tablespoons olive oil
- 1 onion, chopped
- 2 cloves garlic, minced
- 2 carrots, peeled and chopped
- 2 celery stalks, chopped
- 2 potatoes, peeled and chopped
- 2 cups beef broth
- 1 cup red wine (optional)
- 2 tablespoons tomato paste
- 1 teaspoon dried thyme
- 1 teaspoon dried rosemary
- Salt and pepper, to taste
- Chopped fresh parsley, for garnish (optional)

Instructions:

1. In a large pot or Dutch oven, heat the olive oil over medium heat. Add the beef pieces in batches and brown them on all sides. Remove the beef from the pot and set aside.
2. In the same pot, add the chopped onion and minced garlic. Cook until softened and fragrant, about 3-4 minutes.
3. Add the chopped carrots, celery, and potatoes to the pot, and cook for another 5 minutes, stirring occasionally.
4. Return the browned beef to the pot. Pour in the beef broth and red wine (if using), stirring to deglaze the bottom of the pot.
5. Stir in the tomato paste, dried thyme, dried rosemary, salt, and pepper.
6. Bring the stew to a simmer, then reduce the heat to low and cover the pot with a lid. Let the stew simmer gently for 1.5 to 2 hours, or until the beef is tender and the vegetables are cooked through.
7. Taste the stew and adjust the seasoning as needed, adding more salt and pepper if desired.

8. Once the stew is cooked to your liking, remove it from the heat and let it rest for a few minutes before serving.
9. Serve the kiwi beef stew hot, garnished with chopped fresh parsley if desired.

Enjoy your homemade kiwi beef stew as a comforting and satisfying meal, perfect for chilly evenings!

Kiwi Cheese and Bacon Roll

Ingredients:

- 1 sheet puff pastry, thawed
- 200g streaky bacon, cooked until crispy and chopped
- 1 cup grated cheese (such as cheddar or Colby)
- 1 egg, beaten (for egg wash)
- Sesame seeds or poppy seeds (optional, for garnish)

Instructions:

1. Preheat your oven to 200°C (400°F) and line a baking sheet with parchment paper.
2. Roll out the puff pastry sheet on a lightly floured surface into a rectangle, about 0.5cm thick.
3. Sprinkle the chopped bacon evenly over the surface of the puff pastry, leaving a small border around the edges.
4. Sprinkle the grated cheese over the bacon, covering the entire surface of the puff pastry.
5. Starting from one long edge, roll up the puff pastry tightly into a log, like a Swiss roll.
6. Use a sharp knife to slice the puff pastry log into rounds, about 2cm thick.
7. Place the rounds cut side down on the prepared baking sheet, spacing them slightly apart.
8. Brush the tops of the rolls with beaten egg, and sprinkle with sesame seeds or poppy seeds if desired for added flavor and texture.
9. Bake the cheese and bacon rolls in the preheated oven for 15-20 minutes, or until the pastry is golden brown and puffed up.
10. Once baked, remove the rolls from the oven and let them cool slightly before serving.
11. Serve the kiwi cheese and bacon rolls warm as a delicious snack or appetizer, perfect for sharing with family and friends.

Enjoy your homemade kiwi cheese and bacon rolls as a tasty and satisfying treat!

Kiwi Fried Paua

Ingredients:

- 500g fresh paua meat, tenderized and sliced thinly
- 1 cup all-purpose flour
- Salt and pepper, to taste
- 2 eggs, beaten
- 1 cup breadcrumbs
- Vegetable oil, for frying
- Lemon wedges, for serving

Instructions:

1. Tenderize the paua meat by pounding it lightly with a meat mallet or rolling pin. Slice the paua thinly against the grain.
2. Prepare three shallow bowls: one with flour seasoned with salt and pepper, one with beaten eggs, and one with breadcrumbs.
3. Dredge each slice of paua in the seasoned flour, shaking off any excess.
4. Dip the floured paua slices into the beaten eggs, coating them evenly.
5. Press the egg-coated paua slices into the breadcrumbs, ensuring they are well coated on all sides.
6. Heat vegetable oil in a large frying pan or skillet over medium heat.
7. Once the oil is hot, carefully add the breaded paua slices to the pan in batches, making sure not to overcrowd the pan.
8. Fry the paua slices for 1-2 minutes on each side, or until golden brown and crispy.
9. Remove the fried paua slices from the pan and place them on a plate lined with paper towels to drain any excess oil.
10. Repeat the frying process with the remaining paua slices, adding more oil to the pan if needed.
11. Serve the fried paua hot, accompanied by lemon wedges for squeezing over the top.

Enjoy your homemade kiwi fried paua as a delicious appetizer or main dish, showcasing the unique flavors of New Zealand's seafood!

Kiwi Chocolate Fish

Ingredients:

- 200g marshmallows
- 200g milk chocolate (or dark chocolate if preferred)
- 1 tablespoon vegetable oil

Instructions:

1. Line a baking sheet with parchment paper or wax paper.
2. Place the marshmallows in a microwave-safe bowl and microwave them in 30-second intervals, stirring in between, until they are melted and smooth.
3. Using a spoon or spatula, shape the melted marshmallow mixture into fish shapes on the prepared baking sheet. You can make them as big or as small as you like.
4. Once you've shaped all the marshmallow fish, place the baking sheet in the refrigerator for about 30 minutes to firm up.
5. While the marshmallow fish are chilling, melt the chocolate in a heatproof bowl set over a pot of simmering water (double boiler method), or microwave it in 30-second intervals, stirring in between, until smooth.
6. Stir in the vegetable oil into the melted chocolate to help it become smooth and glossy.
7. Remove the marshmallow fish from the refrigerator. Using a fork or dipping tool, dip each marshmallow fish into the melted chocolate, coating it completely.
8. Tap off any excess chocolate and place the chocolate-coated fish back onto the parchment paper-lined baking sheet.
9. Once all the marshmallow fish are coated in chocolate, place the baking sheet back in the refrigerator for another 30 minutes or until the chocolate has set.
10. Once the chocolate has hardened, your kiwi chocolate fish are ready to be enjoyed!

You can store the chocolate fish in an airtight container in the refrigerator for up to a week. Enjoy these delightful treats as a taste of New Zealand's sweet indulgence!